Heart and Stone

HEART
AND
STONE

KATHARINE BITNEY

Turnstone Press

Published with the assistance of the Manitoba Arts Council and the Canada Council.

Turnstone Press
607-100 Arthur Street
Winnipeg, Manitoba
Canada R3B 1H3

This book was printed by Hignell Printing Limited for Turnstone Press.

Cover illustration and design: David Morrow

Printed and bound in Canada

The author gratefully acknowledges a writers' "B" grant from the Manitoba Arts Council.

Earlier versions of some of these poems have appeared, or will be appearing, in *Border Crossings, Poetry Canada Review, Northern Light, CV2, Dandelion, Island,* and *The New Quarterly.*

Canadian Cataloguing in Publication Data

Bitney, Kate
Heart and stone

Poems.
ISBN 0-88801-135-0

I. Title.
PS8553.I75H4 1989 C811'.54 C89-098031-4
PR9199.3.B57H4 1989

To the memory of my father

Jan Wacław Szumigalski
1913-1985

who built the cabin

"La Nature est un temple où de vivants piliers
Laissent parfois sortir de confuses paroles;
L'homme y passe à travers des forêts de symboles
Qui l'observent avec des regards familiers."

Charles Baudelaire, *Correspondances*

Acknowledgements

For their invaluable advice, encouragement and insight, my gratitude to: Andris Taskans, Anne Szumigalski and George Amabile.

Author's Note

These poems are direct and indirect responses to, and meditations on, some of the cards of the Major Arcanum of the Tarot. The poems are informed by contemporary science (particularly quantum physics), metaphysics old and new, and orthodox and heretical theologies. They are also informed by music of many kinds, with the works of J.S. Bach at the top of the list.

The author acknowledges the influence of such poets as Charles Baudelaire, James Merrill, Gwendolyn MacEwen, Robert Allen and Adam Zagajewski, among others.

Contents

Stroke and Void

Heart and Stone

Stroke and Void

Question

In the beginning was the word and the word was bang   or bubble   the word was atom   the word was superstring

In the middle of nothing was this something   this word bang bubble   atom   knot   superball   And before that

In the beginning was this idea that in the middle of nothing there must have been something   because how can there be nothing

In the beginning came the question   why should there be something instead of nothing   The question   what is nothing

And how can there be a beginning if everything occurs in the middle of the question

Why *is* there something instead of nothing   Well there is a void and that is nothing   And in the middle of that void there is this something   this hard ball   this convention of atoms   Atoms are conventions of quarks   protons neutrons and ons and ons

Wait

In the middle of the void is a tiny ball   The ball explodes And the ball   now no longer a ball   but a huge bubble moves outward from its exploding centre and into   the void But the void is nothing

So if the void is nothing and the bubble expands into the void then the bubble expands into nothing   in which case the universe does not exist

I'll start again

In the beginning was the idea and the idea was a little ball but the little ball was already there   so it precedes the idea and there goes the whole ball game

No

The word is the ball   The ball is spoken out of the mouth of God which is a black hole leading to another universe

So

Wholeness and the Implicate Order

The man walking in the desert
strides like Moses
his garments made for sand
visor for eyes
dustpiece at mouth
searching for a friend

His search a string of clues

> *nasturtium*   round nubby pods   lilypad leaves
> the scent of bells in bloom
> love in the hollows of the flower
>
> *water*   unrehearsed flow of a young stream
> sagesse of heavy seas
> rain pool's improvised life
> rapture   necessity
>
> and *topaz*   not the yellow but the blue
> big as a pillow   cut and polished
> inscrutable as insect life   glacier ice

and more words

Now with tired feet
he sits down on the sand
pulls off his sandals
leans against a petrified tree

Does he find his friend   perhaps
the body will wash down an arroyo
perhaps the friend will walk
out of shimmering sand

But he hears the friend's injured mind
sees the face   a hologram   his memory
nasturtium   water   topaz

The man sighs   pulls the desert
back into his eyes

Elijah

As if we could choose   Elijah
the time   the genes   the place
where we are born
how we live   how we die
we're complacent here
the scenes as easy to change
as tv channels

This planet is a rococo balcony
overlooking history
camera circles a bandstand
in dark woods   away from sunny lawns
a gothic murder
the body stuffed into a toolshed
slow dance of figurines

It's never decisive battles
grand gestures that interest us
rather   the little scenes
births   deaths   weddings   a string quartet
the gardener turning soil
a woman bending to hang out clothes
the small heroic gestures   how over time
the wildness of a girl becomes
the discipline of a matron's world

Why is the body so still   Elijah
dreaming in the rose room
breeze drifting through french doors
music fused to molecules of air
the body   if you love it
moves with grace and pleasure
those are the hips
that launched a thousand orgasms
they move like that   Elijah
arms swaying as though boneless
love is graceful in its tiny gestures
each a metaphor   a pregnant word
a pure voice rising from dream

Now look   Elijah
the soldiers thunder by on horseback
all eyes and blazing scimitars
oh the vigour of those days
the horses and the dead
a murder of crows
flapping black rags in the wind

Swimmers

This is the pool
where under a moon of dreams
our swimmers wait
their headlong muscles tensed
at the water's edge
we broadcast from our towers
to the watching world

The gun shouts
our swimmers jump
are swallowed up by blue

From God knows how deep they surface
their trails   curled arcs in pure fluid
we photograph as proof of charm and truth
beam them to earth by satellite

Here come the swimmers
gleaming in aqua light
the winners speed to the end
churn to foam

Now hear the wolves
all that's left
to broadcast from our towers
the swimmers are ghosts
floating up the road
thin radio signals

What You Want

What you want is something pornographic
not myriad lyrics on the afterlife
what you want is what will lift you out
of your four walls
your box   you like to call it
what will lift you like a starship away
from the blue marble world   what
you want you want you want
to write poetry with one hand
make love with the other

Les Amants

The afternoons are convoys
threading the summer months
filling the room with sun
through venetian blinds
soft wind lifts the lovers' breath

Etienne's body shifts   exhales
bright fields of silky grass   scarlet flowers
sun wheel splinters on bending blades
into the cup of dream he scoops
loose particles
they dance there
matter   antimatter

Violet is curled in the arm of sleep
her head releases small blue planets
glass balls that bounce in the bedroom air

Each is a hypothesis
pink wings and seven-sided crystals slide
collapse into a catscradle of shifting light
turning their dreams
with the ease of sunboats
navigating stars

Coma Girl

Your bed floats away
your body sleeps   huge as a planet
near death you turn from marvel to marvel

The doctors flutter and shout
cut and stitch your skin
press ears to your heart
your body an octopus of tubes   you are
blips and bleeps on a screen
turn away   coma girl   and as you leave
leave something burning

Now death is the friend who takes you in
teaches you the alchemy of matter
fine web spun by mind's little spider

Here's the blue angel you've been
sending your heartsick friends
the light that floods from your third eye
here you find the gardens out of fairy tales
the fragrant air   the dangerous blooms
the talking birds with plumes of fire

That demure girl who died at school
sits here reading a book of poetry
Oh Mother   she tells you   I'll come down soon
flicking her light to earth

Now you pass to the sleeping fields
the threshold
death gives you back
to the slow world

where they are visiting you with roses
imagining you ask for a cigarette
you say the ashes drop like shooting stars
you call for a girl named Azure
you're singing in your sleep

Where are my bodies   my skeletons
will they rise   be judged
which will speak for me   clothed
in the final flesh   the shining

My lives are names on stones
crushed bones on battlefields
ziggurats   sandhills
towers of silence

I convene my fossils wherever I choose
to look   where I feel the pull
of death under dark trees
where light makes pictures in sea fog
stone coffins float out to sea
rock on waves from the spacious past
are memories   slide by in dreams
roll   rock away   rock away   roll
these bones are for show
for dancing

You recline on a sunny hill   heady scents
red lilies   yarrow   vetch   tough beauties
and the bees of music make you sleep
the children disappear downhill
to green adventure   their voices
rising from another world   another time
your body floats on their smoke
your bed is a field of fire

Jordan Brown

Jordan Brown dreams of a man in flames
that is me   he thinks
as fire cleans his bones

The man in flames looks back at Jordan Brown
it seems the more he burns
the more he's cleansed
the crowd of spinning heads
Ophanim come to take him home

I am the heretic twisting in the fire
who sees the horrid eyes of Bellarmine
he stands beside the crowd in his carmine robes
around him victory hangs as smoke hangs
on smouldering rags of flesh

The man in flames remembers Jordan Brown
someone in that other world   twisting
in the heat of his wifeless sleep

On a page half-burned with words
Jordan Brown writes down the ashes
of the man in flames

Hologram and Laser

In the middle of your mind
a priestess with a book
tames the moon with her foot
the blue circle of her crown a laser
your third eye splits its light
into pillars   beam and reference beam
behind the priestess   screen   obscuring pool
holograms you make with your mind
body   brain   world

for instance

  a sunny hillside
  children play on the slopes
  they've found an old barn
  are climbing to the loft   a sheer drop
  their world is a place without danger
  they don't understand
  their mother's screams of fear

and/or

  a garden on a rainy day
  the colours   green   chocolate   chestnut
  sparrows chitter in still air
  cats shake off rain
  onions reach for the slate sky

and more

what does the priestess know of your life
in her book it is written
the world is your hologram

The Aerialist

Here is an adept
a different sort of saint
whose view of the world
is never right side up
it is not luck but sanctity
that lets him hang like this
a nimbus clinging
to his dangling hair
look at his smile
the smile of pleasure beyond pain

Mother believes in saints
note   she says   that he hangs
like Jesus from a tree
like Peter   upside down
like Buddha he is untouched
by the accident of life

I look at the card
a thief hanged on a gibbet
head downward
the better to empty his pockets
of stolen gold

The Seven-Sided Self

The carbon soul is gem-strong
passion caged inside the molecule
woman bends like light around it
curls   containing it
with an adept's ease

fire frays her edges
she's white as fox fur
attaching wings to a lion's heavy head

In Dark Matter

The Emperor of Geometry is a prisoner
in his chair   unable to move
speechless beyond slur
lips against teeth
flesh against bone
he's hurtling through space
toward a knot
at the heart of time

Leaning forward in their desks
the students listen to this dizzy voyage
to strange slow gurgles rising
from the place
where language is assembled
the words pile up like Chinese acrobats
    singularity   event horizon
    wave function   particle
    helix   rhombus   trapezoid

and the lines of calculus unbind
into jumbled numbers
tumbling with the Emperor
in dark matter
Draco   the shadow world

from his lips a single bubble
floats   settles on his hand
inside the bubble words and numbers struggle
into arcs   landscapes   pyramids
niagaras   spirals   cones

the audience applauds
this geometric scaffold unfolding
to the fifth and sixth dimensions
the bubble spins
an oscillating universe
balanced perfectly
on one thin hand

Stroke and Void

Into our summer house troop children
smiles worn inside
sister holds brother's hand
both balance a brush
between stroke and void

Together they dream
of bamboo and pole boats
side by side they paint
the hoodoo mountains
their minds wrapped 'round unseen gardens
forests   farmyard animals

They look calmly out square windows
onto the grey streets of Shanghai

Behind them   shadow
of the looming sage
forever contemplating
black ink on white rice paper
with utmost delicacy explaining
order/disorder

The children   always quiet
look down centuries

The Family Dreams in a Scented Gazebo

This is the gazebo where we like to laze
on ozone scented summer afternoons in the garden
Mother   Father   sometimes one child   sometimes another

Our tea cools in the blue teapot   a stray bee
caught with us in the summer house
buzzes flowers painted on our china cups
through the screens drift breezes laced
with peony and rose   opiate air
the colour of the sun
carrying in its subatomic structure
miniature worlds for common dreams

In semi-sleep we piece together a land
a planet of lands   plants of the planet
particles of the plants   exotic scarlet blooms
the size of sheepsheads   mushrooms with pelts
like the backs of fawns

We water them from subterranean pools
clear as mathematics

This is a probable world
we cannot agree on fauna
create incongruous beasts
who'll have to fight for balance

A's dinosaurs will wipe each other out
they always do   while Mother's shrew
will once again triumph

And Father spins his beautiful arachnids
their nets hang gracefully between trees
sagging a little from dew or raindrops
trembling with tiny captured birds

I fail again with the winged men
again they maintain their distance
their liberty between dimensions
no one on any planet
ever finds their skeletons
they slip away from me
it's like banging your head against a wall

I ponder my perennial failure   millenia pass
as we dawdle the afternoon away in the gazebo
weaving and reweaving the webs of worlds

Scaramouche

Of all the cards
the Fool is most like God
innocent
a being of utter faith
he steps off mountains
into the void
eye turned skyward
reading his path's map
from the shifting clouds
look at his guileless smile
the way he moves
without number

God likes to invent stories
about himself   his knapsack
for instance   could hold a fiddle
or a harp   could be a flute
a handkerchief stuffed with symphonies
he pretends the world
is made with every note
paths appear as he walks
clouds as he regards the sky

The world hates God the Fool
for what he is
a madman   a child

Oh Pa   we tell him
act your bloody age

The Habit of Death

It begins like this
a hundred nights dreaming
not of death   but life
as though nothing had happened
I remember these dreams

The moment before release is clear and swift
I feel a rush   the drum of wings
or blood around my ears
and I'm shot   torpedoed
through a red-ribbed tunnel
Suddenly out   I swing
like a monkey to the ceiling
watch without passion the last rites

I don't know what eyes I use
to see myself
a young girl on a bunk bed
reading the lives of saints
a woman crumpled by the phone
steam heat hissing
a soldier in the hospital
one leg missing

Each death has its pleasures
its private jokes
death is a dreamt thing
something you do
each death detailed
a poem

Death is the state of a thousand acts
a bazaar for the shopping soul

The Virtuoso

If you consider the Magician
you see two images
one   God as magician
imagination creating instant change
two   God as magician
reduced to miracles
parlour tricks

are they the same
depends on where you put him in the deck

still there's another name for the card
jongleur   the juggler
that is the god of
  a) the universe as fun and games or
  b) chance   random
for what if he drops the balls
what if he misses his toss

If he's God he won't

And if he's not

Fear of Falling and Dying

The first fear is falling
remembering that flight is impossible
flying   the subtle body
lets time slip
lets gravity idle
while self sails by

True   to the massless soul
this could be ether
or nothing but a wish
a child's desire that it be so
this is no place for up   down   there
anything that mass requires of space
this is a place for light and loop-de-loops
for dolphin leaps
grand whale breaches
here spirit flees inertia
bounds away where space should be

But heart is a magnet
remembering that flight
is impossible
plunges
plummets to flesh
to sanity

Stars

Ringing a single note
the stars uncurl the petals
of the atom's scale   cordella
for making worlds

Sakharov in Exile I

No pen   not a scrap of paper allowed
exit the world   enter utter boredom

On a mental prison wall I stroke off days
count sheep   count injustices
count charged and uncharged particles
measure their thin arcs
the equations will not hold in air
disperse
a blizzard of quarks

Another walk around the block
strolling with Yelena   even in this cold
this closed city   lightens the heart
sullen guards   miffed at the posting
sniff   spit   goosestep in their shiny boots
just to see them stamp their frozen feet
a small satisfaction

One year   two   a hunger strike
no pen   no paper

Sakharov in Exile II

I am not getting any better
the fever runs beneath my blood's current
always there in the flow
always   my head aches slightly
I tire too fast
the appropriate season refuses
to come on time   refuses
to let me out of the body
that fevers   shivers
I get no better   I get no worse

The body is a prison
when I feel well I will say
the body is a prism   and I'll look
through the illusion of flesh
to scatterings of particles
catch them in their rainbow dance
I will say   the body is a metaphor
for light in context   sound in order
mind in ecstasy   I'll say
this body is my creation
I am its god

My wife is sympathetic
it's better to be ill when you're imprisoned
you haven't the energy to resist
you fail to notice bars   the locks   the guards
someone else will watch the door
care if the mail comes uncensored
shut the bedroom window on cold nights
I don't care
my wife can have the bother

Sakharov Meets Nikola Tesla in a Dream

At first I see only a figure   cross-shaped
still as a statue   decorated top to toe
with pigeons   the figure turns
they followed me through death
says the prophet Tesla
pigeons   blessed birds

Tesla has brought his whole lab
metal balls bounce on copper tubes
lightning thrashes
blueprints leap from his head
from his fingers new machines
shoot sparks
his mind a Tokyo of lights and traffic

I would rather dream of slender women
draped under Chinese lamps
but here is Tesla   elegant in evening suit
pointing like a god to the machinery
of earthquake   thunderstorm

Tesla in a cloud chamber
clouds are pigeons
roosting on his arms and head
if he is quiet they feed from his hands
tell him the secrets of the universe

In Gorky there are no pigeons
clouds are only clouds
rain   snow   so much snow
if I stand in the street
stretch out my arms
will snowflakes settle on me
like Tesla's birds

Cantata

When snow falls there is always music rising
each flake a note   each handful a motet
the crystals ringing against each other
falling on roofs   burying everything

like the pure girls I never understood
snowfall is death   the other world intruding
a light left on after the house is closed

white is a diaphonic chant
drifting in mountain wind
girls singing   blossoms of ice
the ash of hearts gone ages
now falling back to earth
cantatas of white white white

is for innocence
snow gathers into a goddess
her skirt is spruce forest
white is her voice
eddying in wind

is hair falling everywhere
earth the shoulders of pure girls
looking up
singing death to ashes
the other world intruding

Heart and Stone

Bach

The moon is missing
morning lights a page
is turned by a delicate hand
sleeved in fraying lace

A kitten pounces on a mouse
a wife adjusts her cap
the maid with a bowl of milk
steps sturdily up stone
to the chiarascuro kitchen

The kitten crosses the open clavier
scatters clangs and tinkles
into window light   spinning out
great glass roses

In the parlour a young man bows his cello
certain of his way in fading light
and evening falls on the hands
that execute those easy loops
those perfect sprays on clouds

When Father returns to the haloed house
the children lift their violins and play
andante summer days in the tangled garden
the players' hands are happy spiders

This is why we take on flesh   says Mama
Father nods his head and folds his hands
still warm with the memory of flight over organ keys
his heart still booming with the pipes

Heavy Metal in Hot Weather

Day and night we dream the drums
pressed to the ground we smell
the ozone edge   storms tease us
with their delicious war
snake-tongued lightning
steaming bodies
we can't take much more of this

Lift us to the booming clouds
where heaven jerks its hips
Lord give us thunder
give us rock 'n' roll
we'll dance like Zulus
we'll elope with the air

Himself

Here comes the devil
king in his crown of horns
lord of the lusty forest
moves on the ground that loves him
father of secrets   father of things
burns whom he chooses
keeps the living world
always young and in peril

Here comes the naughty god
shaming the pious
with his lies of hell
lover of the juicy earth
in spring the devil jigs
with the jumping fox
but in winter woods slinks
silver as frosted trees

At the Cabin

Always it's Christmas
the coloured lights
in our cabin burn all night
the fluted trees exhale soprano frost
and the sky is white or wedgewood
indigo at night
at four o'clock
the salmon sun declines
but we stay up
the children ski to lake's end
voices floating to tree tops
beyond

Indoors   a dozen pairs of boots and mitts
festoon the stove
hour upon hour we stare
into the leaping fire
sip brandy out of camping cups
winter is the landscape
of our dreams these nights
moon and stars ice-sharp
ice-bright

Our tenor hunters tramp about the bush
each morning   heroes of the rabbit hunt
scanning the placid snow
for one pink eye or ear
one movement
of the pure white snowshoe hare
one a day we collect them
for a feast at holiday's end

Northern Lights

Now the light dies down
the children doze
like dogs by the fire
we speak in low voices
about the Wheel of Fortune
and these times

Mother says
wheel is a clock   a universe
seasons spun
by the steady hand of God
the wheel turns
and we with it
here in the north
we spin at a higher speed
we move off the world
the wheel moves on

I recall those overpowering stars
sky a crystal bowl that covered us
a wheel of lights and tones
Balinese gongs   Tibetan bells

Father scoffs
potters spun the first wheel
sold it to men with practical needs
warriors   tradesmen   travellers
farmers   priests
witness calendars   coins   clocks
engines of industry   chariots of war
wheel steers ships   trucks   convoys
wheel is the shape of cheese

The children stir
their sleep balloons out
orbits of earth and moon
spiral galaxies whizz 'round the room
bells   satellites   flying saucers
medicine wheels
phonograph discs on a flywheel
playing the Rolling Stones

Chariot Rock

He's got a big guitar   hangs
below his belt   he bangs
the strings to stardust
he does the hippy shake
doo-wop girls up front
drummer drums the wheels

When he struts   his hair swings
like a horse tail   brushes
the heads on both his shoulders
hair of a lion   hair of a king

He's got a microphone
big as a battle sword
when he shoves it at the crowd
the girls all scream and swoon

what did he say
was he singing to me
who was that anyway
rockin' round the universe
doin' the Chariot Rock

War Memory

I see the burning plane
as a hawk might see
an injured rabbit in a field

Curious   how it's twisted
tossed from the sky
upended

the mangled pilot wears his cockpit
broken armour hanging
on an unhorsed knight   alarmed
I soar down   drag the body out

I turn him over
our skull empties onto the sand

Why Whales Founder on Beaches

Whales are Buddhists   sorrowing
for birds sucked into jet engines
for the taming of orcas and porpoises
for mutilated creatures in science labs
grotesque cancers incubated on tiny rats
kittens with their eyes sewn shut
do you imagine the whales don't know

from time to time
they hurl themselves on beaches
to die
why
because they are disgusted

Whales die conspicuously
crushed by their own weight
it's an ugly death
an uglier disintegration
those huge bodies rot
for months on sand
there are too few scavengers
to spare the locals the smell

Resurrection

Nothing ever stays dead
no resurrection is final
no body comes back the same
no body leaves the way it came

Death is an alchemist   Death is a gardener
Death moves to the currents of earth
Watch the seasons
if you don't believe me

You cannot tell gardener Death his business
can't say what he carries is a hoe or scythe
resurrection is not a body snatched from Death
who is economical and likes no waste
no theft   no nonsense

Resurrection is a new spring hat
watch the ladies on the street
if you don't believe me
resurrection is a spade in the dirt
watch the gravediggers
if you don't believe me
resurrection is the same thing every time
we are sure it will come
we are amazed when it does

The Sun

When they leave   do they ever come back
trailing jasmine   ribbons of birds
do they ever ride back on their pale ponies
an armful of babies
a diary of the places they have been

was it Tibet
yes Mother   I grew to manhood there
in a stony town   a garden of rhododendron
Oh Mother how you would have loved it
sometimes I leaned from the window
of my smoky hut   and dreamed of you

and I dreamed of you
of the day you spurred the horse
and flew   flinging back
your fat baby laugh

your greetings came
from places where you grew
pictures of a wheel   a cat
a fierce woman in fur
such words   such language
today the warrior   tomorrow
the toast of Paris Underground

I pin these photos
to a corkboard in my room
souvenirs of lives
I hope to lead

Colouring Your Hand

This is the jewel   the one
everyone's been looking for
this one   the red one
the one you've been looking for
and it fits in your hand perfectly
you see it colouring your hand
cupped perfectly around it

Now that you've found it
what will you do
more than that   why
did you want it

Madonnas

Where the ancient goddess goes
her ample garment billows
in the afternoon's light breeze
her bodice loose
and bosom mobile
the twelve stars of heaven her tiara

she keeps her lovers to herself
holds them   sceptres   to her crown

hides matters of life and death
under the easy print of her frock

my women friends are pagans
lounging on the loose edge
their lovers are cruel men
hard in the right places
are names whispered over the phone
or breathed into the heavy dark
of sharp staccato sex

Purple Irises

As complex as an orchid
iris droops its purple lips
and lolls a yellow tongue

spears whose heads explode
as royal genitalia   bobbing   leering
they rear their serpent necks
to mock the puritan gardener

Yes   an impure plant
a vulgar flower   hybrid whore
of complicated blossoms in a jar
a six pack of vegetable sex

She Writes to Him from Tibet

Dearest   but for the snow
filling up mountains
everything here is empty
an exile
I fear your burning eyes
can't remember strength
when I think of your tongue
kissing my hand   my wrist
sex   sin   salvation   are these for us
we were written into history
as pictures on a card
yet in these cold rooms
I feel your heat   your power

and how my power fails
in the wake of love
you can imagine my dreams
pushing my tongue into your cleft lip
losing my hands in your hair
finding your stain
on my magician's gown

My nimbus slips
draws us into its figure eight
either we are the figure
or we are caught
embryos in adjacent wombs
could we twist
the figure into a disc
a flying saucer
a flat crystal of snow
coming to rest
on the roof of the world

Atahualpa

The priest turns from light
pushes an acolyte away
let it be simple
he begs the gods
who burden him
with knives of sacrifice

I have nothing to reveal
this tower is only stone
and blood   words on stone
show me what makes mind jump
heart dizzy as dancers' feet

Looking out to no horizon
the priest puts hand to eye
breeze shivers his feather crown
stirs folds in his perfect turquoise gown
the brilliant mountains sound to him
like wind in reeds
breath in the wooden flute
uphill winds a passion of girls
bright birds with their cargo
of colour and innocence

Arguing Raven's Case

The prosecution rests
I stand for Raven
arguing her case against the gun
the stair   the car keys   blood on a dress
the room where there was murder

Raven hides nothing
not her loves nor her diamonds
she is a bird of high spirits
is   if you like   what she does
jetting to Morocco
the sacred rubies
red eyes in the temple dark

You are imagining the crime
your minds dark with guns
the body stranded
between death and discovery
your hearts go out to that bewildered ghost
fluttering in shock around the room
the tableau waiting for the police
Raven fleeing in a red sports car

But who is the killer
shadow in the darkened room
hunter   spurned lover
slave fleeing from another planet
robber startled in his crime
this is your murderer
Raven only sees and shares the spoils

Heart and Stone

Panting up frost clouds
Heart and Stone run to the hunt
Raven flies with us
through her eyes I see
the ibex on a rise

forest soaks up clamour and blood
we fell the generous beast
Stone to throat   Heart tearing out heart
the eyes go to Raven

by night we cluster near fire
sky pours its white kindness
snow for light and pleasure
Heart and Stone smile in their sleep

I carry flames deep into the cave
the creatures I love stand here on rock
Bison   Horse   Ibex   Lion   Wolf
my dogs excluded

fire flares on the walls
I peer into the mind of another man who walks
exactly where I walk
we move through the cave   one man
he's stunned at my pictures
heart on stone
I should set my dogs on him
for what he's thinking
that I can't pray
can't fill my sleep with angels

my hands amaze that man
with what I know
where the gods hunt
the forest green and white
my black dogs running with me

Midsummer Night I

Past midnight
spirits wake me   lead me to the window
where I kneel   lean my elbows on the sill
I am five and well prepared

In the farmhouse the others sleep
Mother   Father   Sister
they don't see the gauzy apparitions
dancing on the lawn
don't see me float to the ground
my gown a parachute
my hair a parasol

I'm caught at the centre of a blurry sphere
of Druid children   spirits
of the European woods
they whirl and I am sucked
down their dance

leaving at the window
an alien child

Cat's Play

In the window my cat washes her grey fur
a coat of sound surrounds her like a glory
she raises up her purr
rolls it down her flat skull
knowing what the world is made of

Kitty sleeps   smiles
the wise smile of cats
pats fire into balls
with her quick paws
tosses a jumble of stars into orbit
sets spinning the wheels of galaxies

she dreams up emperors
philosophers and gods
the poet hanging
in his metaphysical sleep

gives them all away
for a plate of chicken bones

Midsummer Night II

Tonight the cats will not be touched
or spoken to

the neighbour's dog stops for once his whining

planets beam unusually bright

a bat flaps low over the roof

and while you look away south
where Jupiter is brilliant
two rival satellites cross paths above us
travelling east in flawless arcs

guessing at stars
we stand at the world's centre
feet bare on the blue lawn
you point out Andromeda
the Big Dipper

and if tonight we were your ancestors
our sky would blaze from pitch torches
raised high in the evening fields

all *Jāņi* we revellers would sing
dance   get drunk on heavy mead

this morning we lie scattered
sleeping in the dew
the old gods with us
Laima   *Austra*   *Pērkons*
Māra   *Jumis*   *Auseklis*
farmers   marriers   progenitors
air thick with their descent

Love Poem

Everywhere else it seemed impossible
but here we are only a man and woman in love
we can pull down planets
disconnect the moon

Stars turn over us in their arcs
the field is starred with summer flowers
those that open at night
those that never close
you hold my hand as you always do   cupped
loose in the shelter of your hand

Your eyes pull me down
the distance that was a galaxy
between us   gone nova
collapsed into nothing by
what air can squeeze between us

What You Are in Dance

You whirl around   see me watching
your honey hair swings one way
your honey hips   the other
boots to the carpet
breaking out sparks

What you are in dance   pure light
drums shake your particles apart
they fling away
not wanting to come in
from the fields
the sun   the flowers
their dancing heads

Ballerina of the World

Mother fans the cards
selects this final one   The World
The secrets of the universe are here
At the centre of the world the dance of fire

fire at the centre of the elliptical world
mandorla   not mandala   here
the ballerina spins   dancer   androgyne
two-wanded majorette   wand tips aflame

the universe rolls out   not into space
but making it   as thought
rolls out the universe
the substance of the world

is the whirl of thought   the leap of minds
the rock and roll of dream
the smoke of Heaven's fire
rolls out and in
a waltz of Heaven's dreams

Here Mother sways her hand like cloth
catching air

the world   she says   is this and this and this

and nothing more